HOLIDAYS, FESTIVALS, & CELEBRATIONS

MOTHER'S DAY

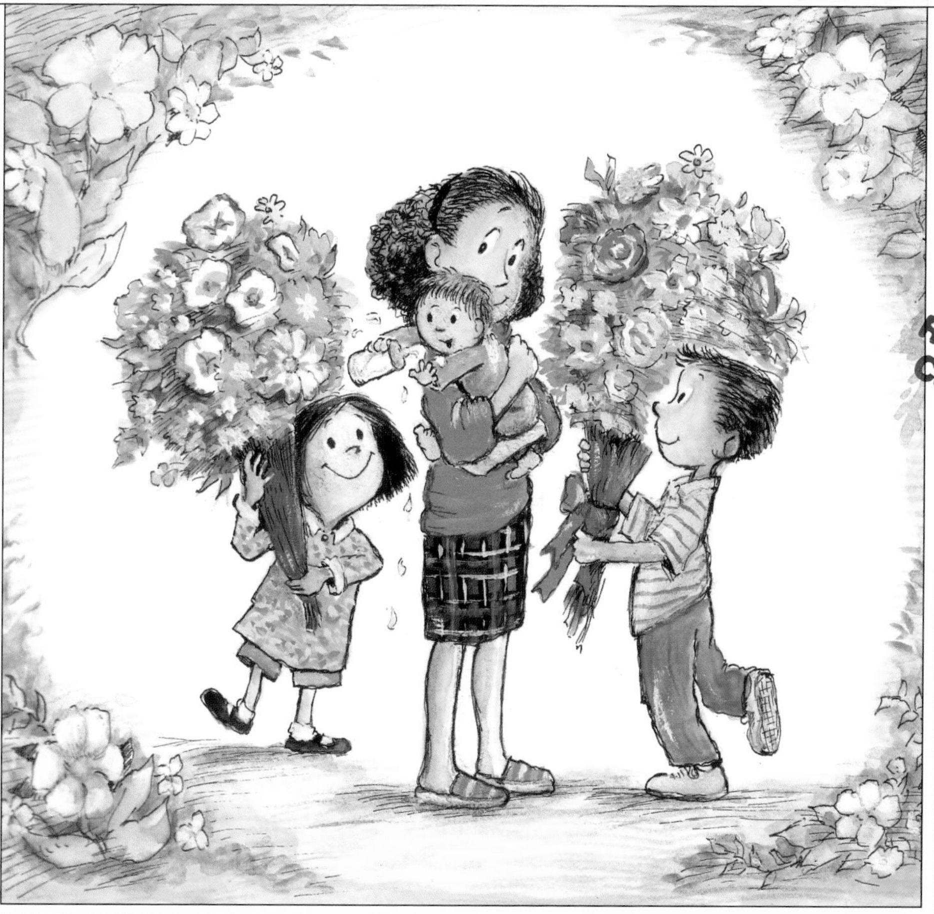

BY ANN HEINRICHS · ILLUSTRATED BY R. W. ALLEY

The Child's World

Published in the United States of America by The Child's World®
PO Box 326 • Chanhassen, MN 55317-0326
800-599-READ • www.childsworld.com

ACKNOWLEDGMENTS
The Child's World®: Mary Berendes, Publishing Director

Editorial Directions, Inc.: E. Russell Primm, Editorial Director; Katie Marsico, Managing Editor; Judith Shiffer, Assistant Editor; Caroline Wood and Rory Mabin, Editorial Assistants; Susan Hindman, Copy Editor and Proofreader; Elizabeth Nellums, Rory Mabin, Ruth Martin, and Caroline Wood, Fact Checkers; Tim Griffin/IndexServ, Indexer

The Design Lab: Kathleen Petelinsek, Design and Page Production

LIBRARY OF CONGRESS CATALOGING-IN-PUBLICATION DATA
Heinrichs, Ann.
Mother's Day / by Ann Heinrichs ; illustrated by R. W. Alley.
p. cm. — (Holidays, festivals, & celebrations)
Includes index.
ISBN 1-59296-579-2 (library bound : alk. paper)
1. Mother's Day—Juvenile literature. I. Alley, R. W. (Robert W.), ill. II. Title. III. Series.
HQ759.2.H45 2006
E394.2628—dc22 2005025686

TABLE OF CONTENTS

CHAPTER ONE

HAPPY MOTHER'S DAY!

Who ran to help me when I fell,
And would some pretty story tell,
Or kiss the place to make it well?
My Mother.
—"My Mother" by Ann Taylor

What do you call your mother? Mother, Mama, Mommy, or Mom? Whatever you call her, she's very special. That's why we have a holiday just for her. It's Mother's Day!

That day, we thank mothers for all they do. We also celebrate those who are like mothers to us. They may be grandmothers, aunts, **stepmothers**, or sisters.

What's the best way to say "Happy Mother's Day"? Just say, "I love you!"

Mother's Day is time to show mothers how much we love them.

CHAPTER TWO

CELEBRATING MOTHERHOOD

Many ancient religions had a mother goddess. Her festivals were often in the spring. Crops were sprouting then. And flowers were bursting into bloom. It was a time to rejoice in new life.

Ancient Romans honored Cybele (SIH-buh-lee). They saw her as the mother of the gods. Cybele's festival took place in March. Dancers whirled around as the music played. We may not celebrate so wildly today. But we still honor our mothers!

A man's work is from sun to sun, but a mother's work is never done.
—Author unknown

Ancient Romans used music and dance to celebrate Cybele.

CHAPTER THREE

A SUNDAY FOR MOTHERS

Mothering Sunday began long ago in England. Poor children often lived away from home. They worked as servants for rich people.

Every spring, servants got a day off. They were to attend their mother church. That was the church in their hometown. The day was called Mothering Sunday.

Children looked forward to Mothering Sunday. They missed their families. And they really missed their mothers!

The children hurried down the sunny lanes. Along the way, they stopped to pick wildflowers.

Mothering Sunday is the fourth Sunday during Lent. Lent is a traditional Christian season before Easter.

Why? To give to their mothers! In time, Mothering Sunday became a holiday to honor mothers.

Mothering Sunday was an early version of Mother's Day.

A mother's arms are made of tenderness, and children sleep soundly in them.
—Victor Hugo
(1802–1885)

CHAPTER FOUR

HOW DID MOTHER'S DAY BEGIN?

What about our own Mother's Day? It began with Anna Jarvis.

Anna dearly loved her mother. Her mother had started a women's club. Its members helped the sick. They believed in kindness and peace.

Sadly, Anna's mother died in 1905. Anna wanted to honor her mother. She worked hard to create a mothers' holiday. At last, Anna's dream came true. Mother's Day became a **national** holiday in 1914!

In the United States, Mother's Day is celebrated on the second Sunday in May.

Anna Jarvis helped make Mother's Day a national holiday.

Of all the special joys in life,
The big ones and the small,
A mother's love and tenderness
Is the greatest of them all.
—Author unknown

CHAPTER FIVE

HOW DO WE CELEBRATE?

We celebrate Mother's Day by showing moms how much we love them.

There are many Mother's Day traditions. We may give our mother a greeting card. Mother's Day cards are very pretty. Inside is a special, loving message. We might give her flowers, too. Candy is another favorite gift. It shows how sweet she is!

Many people wear a **carnation** on Mother's Day. A red or pink carnation means the mother is living. A white carnation means she has died. But a child's love for her lives on.

Once upon a memory
Someone wiped away a tear,
Held me close and loved me—
Thank you, Mother dear.
—Author unknown

Cards, candy, flowers, and kisses are all good Mother's Day gifts!

My mother had a great deal of trouble with me, but I think she enjoyed it.
—Mark Twain
(1835–1910)

CHAPTER SIX

PRESIDENTS AND THEIR MOTHERS

My mother was the most beautiful woman
I ever saw. All I am I owe to my mother.
—*George Washington, first president*

There never was a woman like her. She was
gentle as a dove and brave as a lioness.
—*Andrew Jackson, seventh president*

All that I am or ever hope to be,
I owe to my angel mother.
—*Abraham Lincoln, sixteenth president*

U.S. presidents often wrote about their respect and admiration for their mothers.

No mother has an easy time, [and]
most mothers have very hard times.
—Theodore Roosevelt, twenty-sixth president

U.S. presidents were first their mothers' sons!

No one in the world can take
the place of your mother. Right or wrong,
from her viewpoint you are always right.
—*Harry Truman, thirty-third president*

Former president Harry Truman knew how special mothers are.

CHAPTER SEVEN

MOTHER'S DAY AROUND THE WORLD

Many countries honor mothers on a special day. In Mexico, Mother's Day is *Día de las Madres* (DEE-ah day lahs MAH-drays). It's always on May 10. Schoolchildren put on dance shows for their mothers. Then everyone enjoys a big meal.

Mother's Day in France is *Fête des Mères* (FEHT day MEHR). It falls on the last Sunday in May. Families gather for a holiday dinner. Then they give Mother a beautiful cake. It's decorated to look like flowers!

Serbian people in Eastern Europe celebrate

God could not be everywhere, so he created mothers.
—Jewish proverb

In France, mothers celebrate their special day with a cake that looks like flowers.

Materice (mah-tehr-EET-say). It's the second Sunday before Christmas. That morning, children tiptoe into their mother's bedroom. They gently tie her up. Then they say, "Mother's Day, Mother's Day. What will you pay to get away?" She promises them gifts she has hidden under her pillow. Giggling with delight, they set her free!

In Serbia, children get gifts on Mother's Day!

CHAPTER EIGHT

THE POETS' CORNER

The Hand That Rocks the Cradle Is the Hand That Rules the World

Blessings on the hand of women!
Angels guard its strength and grace,
In the palace, cottage, hovel,
Oh, no matter where the place;
Would that never storms assailed it,
Rainbows ever gently curled;
For the hand that rocks the cradle
Is the hand that rules the world.

—William Ross Wallace
(1819–1881)

The Reading Mother

You may have tangible *wealth untold;*
Caskets of jewels and coffers of gold.
Richer than I you can never be—
I had a Mother who read to me.

—Strickland Gillilan
(1869–1954)

A Mother's Love

A Mother's love is something
That no one can explain,
It is made of deep devotion
And of sacrifice and pain,
It is endless and unselfish
And enduring come what may
For nothing can destroy it
Or take that love away.

—Helen Steiner Rice
(1900–1981)

Mother

You filled my days with rainbow lights,
Fairy tales and sweet dream nights,
A kiss to wipe away my tears,
Gingerbread to ease my fears.
You gave the gift of life to me
And then in love, you set me free.
I thank you for your tender care,
For deep warm hugs and being there.
I hope that when you think of me
A part of you, you'll always see.

—Author unknown

Showing Our Love on Mother's Day

- Your mother makes meals for you every day. How about serving her breakfast in bed?
- Write a poem or letter to your mother. Begin with "I Love You Because . . ." It can be a very long list!
- Do you have a special grandmother, stepmother, aunt, or sister? Show your love by giving her flowers or a card.
- Do you know someone from another country? Ask if he or she celebrates a special holiday for mothers. Ask what the holiday customs are.
- Is there a home for older people in your community? See if you can visit on Mother's Day. Bring cards or flowers for the women. Ask them to tell you about their lives.
- Try out a new idea: Every day is a day to show Mom how much you appreciate her!

MOM

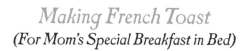

Making French Toast

(For Mom's Special Breakfast in Bed)

Ingredients:

2 eggs
¾ cup milk
½ teaspoon vanilla
1 teaspoon sugar
6 slices of bread
Cooking spray
Fresh strawberries

Directions:

Mix the eggs, milk, vanilla, and sugar in a bowl. Using a fork, whisk (stir quickly) the ingredients. Dip each slice of bread into the mixture so that both sides are coated. Spray a skillet with cooking spray, and allow it to preheat on the stove top for a few seconds. Using tongs or a spatula, place one slice of bread on the skillet. Occasionally turn the bread over, and continue cooking until each side is golden brown. Repeat with the other five slices. Finally, arrange the French toast on a plate, and top with sliced strawberries. Bring your breakfast creation to your mom in bed. Be sure to share with the rest of your family, too!

**Have an adult help you operate the stove.*

Making a Mother's Day Gift Box

Here's a gift your mom is sure to love on her special day.

What you need:

A shoe box or other small box
Markers, paints, crayons, stickers, wrapping paper, and glitter for decorating
Paper
Glue
Small wrapped presents (some examples: coupons for help around the house, candy, tea bags, small soaps, cards)
Ribbon

Instructions:

1. Decorate the outside of the box using markers, paint, crayons or any of the other decorating supplies you choose.
2. Fill the box with the small presents you have chosen.
3. Write a schedule for when you would like her to open each gift. This will be easy if you label each gift with a number.
4. Put the cover on the box and tie it closed with a ribbon.

Now you're ready for a day filled with gift-giving fun. Happy Mother's Day!

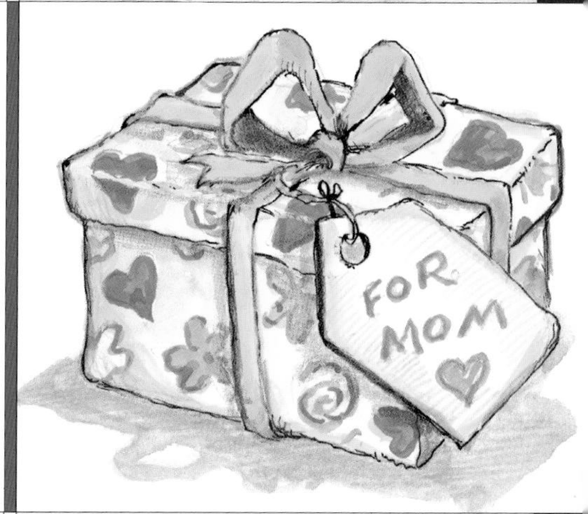

Words to Know

ancient ***(AYN-shunt)*** from the distant past

carnation ***(kar-NAY-shun)*** a flower with fluffy petals

goddess ***(GAH-duss)*** a female god

national ***(NA-shuh-nuhl)*** relating to a country

proverb ***(PRAH-vuhrb)*** a wise saying

stepmothers ***(STEP-muh-thurz)*** women who become mothers after marrying men who already have children

tangible ***(TAN-juh-bull)*** touchable; made of material things

traditional ***(truh-DISH-uh-null)*** following long-held customs

How to Learn More about Mother's Day

At the Library

Balian, Lorna. *Mother's Mother's Day.* New York: Star Bright Books, 2004.

Erlbach, Arlene, and Herbert Erlbach. *Mother's Day Crafts.* Berkeley Heights, N.J.: Enslow Elementary, 2005.

Ruelle, Karen Gray. *Mother's Day Mess.* New York: Holiday House, 2003.

Vail, Rachel, and Steve Björkman. *Mama Rex and T: The (Almost) Perfect Mother's Day.* New York: Scholastic Inc., 2002.

On the Web

Visit our home page for lots of links about Mother's Day:

http://www.childsworld.com/links

NOTE TO PARENTS, TEACHERS, AND LIBRARIANS:

We routinely verify our Web links to make sure they're safe, active sites—so encourage your readers to check them out!

ABOUT THE AUTHOR

Ann Heinrichs lives in Chicago, Illinois. She has written more than two hundred books for children. She loves traveling to faraway places.

ABOUT THE ILLUSTRATOR

R. W. Alley enjoys drawing pictures of happy families from his home in Rhode Island. He's guided in this effort by his winsome wife and two cheery children.

Index